Celtic Mythology

Enchanting Tales of the Ancient World

Isaiah Covington

©Copyright 2021 by Cascade Publishing

All rights reserved.

It is not legal to reproduce, duplicate, or transmit any part of this document in either electronic means or in printed format. Recording of this publication is strictly prohibited.

Table of Contents

Introduction 1

Chapter One: Hudden and Dudden and Donald O'Neary 2

Chapter Two: Master and Man 16

Chapter Three: The Black Thief and the Knight of the Glen 28

Chapter Four: The Fairy Nurse 47

Chapter Five: The Believing Husbands 53

Chapter Six: Connla and the Fairy Maiden 62

Chapter Seven: The Changeling 66

Conclusion 69

Introduction

Folklore and mythology from around the world give us unique insight into how the people of the time viewed the world around them. While this provides us with some historical perspective, after being passed down from generation to generation and then reworked into literature, certain elements can get lost along the way.

This is especially true when reading through the stories that were circulated by word-of-mouth rather than the written word. Because of this, sections that were intended to be acted out or considered universal knowledge were assumed or omitted altogether.

That is why the tales you are about to read have been retooled – but not altered – to allow for better readability and understanding. Each story has been given a new life that will hopefully ignite your curiosity to delve deeper into this world of myth and legend.

Never stop expanding your world – and this is a great place to start!

Chapter One:

Hudden and Dudden and Donald O'Neary

Once, a very long time ago, there were two farmers; one named Hudden, the other named Dudden. They did not lack for anything; they had chickens across their yards, sheep in every field, and herds of cattle in the meadow near the river. Despite all these possessions, Hudden and Dudden were never pleased.

Between the farms of Hudden and Dudden was a small strip of land owned by a man called Donald O'Neary. He was a poor man, having only a hovel to shelter him, a strip of grass that was nearly bare, and one meager cow named Daisy. Due to the harsh conditions, Donald rarely saw any milk from the old girl who had almost no grass to gnaw on.

Looking at all that Hudden and Dudden had to their names, and then glaring over to what little Donald O'Neary called his own, you wouldn't see anything that the two wealthy farmers would have to be jealous of, but you would be wrong.

For as it usually goes, the more one has, the more one ends up wanting. And so it came to be that Hudden and Dudden would spend their days and nights trying to contrive a plot that would allow them to take all of what Donald owned; his shack, his land, and even his starving, scrawny cow, Daisy. Day in and day out the greedy pair would plot and scheme, but nothing ever came of it.

It was on a particularly cruel day that Hudden and Dudden met, muttering and cursing about what Donald had. One would say something like, "This country would be all the better if it was rid of this Donald O'Neary!", prompting the other to agree and respond in kind.

At last, Hudden said firmly, "We need him to leave his land, and what better way to remove his desire to stay than to kill Daisy, his old cow! If that doesn't do it, then nothing will!"

Dudden agreed and the two decided to wait until nightfall.

Once the sun had fully set and the night was upon them, Hudden and Dudden quietly made their way to the sad little shed where Donald kept Daisy at night. They found poor Daisy lying there, trying her best to fill her belly despite there being barely enough grass to even fill the palm of your hand. By the time Donald came out to check on her for the night, Hudden and Dudden had completed their evil deed. Daisy had only seconds left to lick Donald's hand before she closed her eyes and passed.

As you can imagine, Donald was dreadfully heart-broken. Being the shrewd businessman he was, Donald knew that he had to find some good in the death of his Daisy. Through the night, he paced and he paced, and he thought and he thought, until he came to a conclusion. Working hard until dawn, Donald finally set off down the main road towards the city market with the skin of Daisy thrown over his shoulder, a determined look, and every single coin he had jingling with each step.

Just a little ways off from reaching the market, Donald paused by the side of the road. Taking a small knife he then cut several small slices into the cow skin and inside each slit, he placed one of his coins. After looking the skin up and down, he draped it back over his shoulder and continued on his way down the road.

When Donald finally reached the city, he headed straight for the busiest inn he could find, walked inside like he owned the place, found a nail in the wall, and hurled Daisy's skin right up on that nail. Then, calm as he could be, he turned to everyone in the inn, crossed his arms, and sat down in front of the skin hanging from the wall.

Raising his hand, he called out, "Whiskey! The best you've got!"

A tall man poked his head out from behind the bar, giving Donald a look over. Displeased with Donald's commotions, the innkeeper didn't seem all that keen to oblige.

"If you're worried about getting paid for it from the likes of me, you've nothing to be afraid of!" Donald continued, meeting the innkeeper's gaze. "In fact, I've got all the money I could ever need right *here!*"

He motioned emphatically to Daisy's hide hanging behind him. The innkeeper looked even more sure that this ridiculous man was not to be trusted, so Donald gave the skin a hefty smack and out popped a penny. Instantly, the innkeeper's eyes grew wide and he scurried out from the back.

"That skin there, how much you want for it?" asked the innkeeper, hands wringing in anticipation of the riches he would possess.

"*My* skin hanging here? No, no, sir, that is not for sale," Donald responded, shaking his head slowly to add emphasis.

"Let's say I offer one whole gold piece?" the innkeeper pressed further.

Donald didn't even look up from the table. "She's not for sale, my good man, I've already told you. Why would I give away the means that has kept my family in wealth for so long?" And as he finished, he gave the skin another hit, sending another coin flipping out into his hand. "Not for sale, sir."

This exchange went back and forth for some time until, at last, Donald influenced the innkeeper up to quite the exorbitant sum. After the sale had been made, Donald O'Neary set off on the road back home with both pockets and belt jingling with gold.

Before Donald returned home, he wandered over to Hudden's doorway. After a moment of knocking, Hudden appeared and was beyond surprised to see Donald of all people standing before him with a grin spread from ear to ear.

"My good sir, Hudden," Donald began with a flourish. "You have sets of scales with which to weigh your wealth. Would you lend me the best you own?"

Hudden could only blink in confusion before retreating to fetch his best scales. In what seemed like another opportune moment, Hudden concocted a devious plan that would allow him another chance to steal from O'Neary.

As quietly as can be, Hudden spread butter on one of the scales, then hurried back to Donald. After bidding Donald farewell, he raced across the fields to Dudden's farm where he found Dudden sitting on the porch. Huffing and puffing, Hudden told him of Donald borrowing the scales and the butter he spread over them.

"Now we just wait, my friend," said Hudden.

Donald made it home safely, and only when he was sure that he was alone, did he pour out the gold from his holdings. After he set up the scales, he began weighing the gold in piles, then setting them aside. Through the night, he counted and weighed until the sun began to rise and took the last stack from the scales, setting them with the scores of others he had compiled. What Donald didn't know was that there was a single gold piece stuck within the butter that Hudden had spread the night before.

That morning, he went to Hudden to return the scales. With the scales in hand, Hudden ran as fast as he could toward Dudden's. He grabbed his friend and pulled him indoors before setting the scales on the table, letting them both see the sparkling gold piece stuck to the butter.

"You got this from–" began Dudden.

"Donald O'Neary, yes," Hudden replied.

"Donald O'Neary," they both said, eyes fixated on the gold gleaming in the butter.

"And this is just *one* piece!" Dudden cried.

"He must be weighing fistfuls of gold!"

"Sackfuls, even!"

"I've half a mind to go find out what's going on with all this gold and Donald O'Neary!" Hudden loudly said as he stood from the table.

Before they knew it, they were both marching to Donald's in a huff. The further they walked, the angrier they got until they finally arrived at his door.

Inside the small shack, Donald was sitting down recounting the already-counted piles of gold, finding that every time he reached the end his tally seemed to be off. He had no idea that the missing gold piece was stuck to the scales.

Suddenly, the door burst open and in rushed Hudden and Dudden.

"Good evening, Hudden. Good evening, Dudden," he said to them calmly. "You must be wondering how this all came to be! Well, you thought you had gotten the better of me, didn't you? Killing my poor, sweet Daisy; it was meant to be the worst thing to ever happen to me, and yet you have done me the biggest favor ever!" He paused, letting the confusion sink in even deeper for the two men standing in his doorway. "After Daisy's sad passing, I decided to try and find some good in her death, and so I set out for the market with her skin, hoping to fetch enough coin to help my weak bones last a bit longer."

Hudden and Dudden both looked skeptical. They had seen Daisy and her wretched state, and found it highly doubtful that her thin hide had fetched anything at the market, let alone the copious amount of gold Donald had been counting.

"Ah, I see the doubt in your eyes, my friends," O'Neary continued, chuckling a bit. "I was as shocked as you, but hides are worth their full weight in gold!"

Dudden winked at Hudden and the two departed with a new scheme to accrue some more gold for themselves. As they walked off down the path, Donald stood in his doorway and shouted after them, "Have a good evening, my kind friends!"

When dawn arrived the next morning, Hudden and Dudden set off for the market with their wagon filled with the skins of every single cow, calf, and bull they owned. Cruel grins spanning the width of their faces as the pair anticipated their riches. The journey was long and tiresome indeed considering the load. It took four of their strongest horses to even pull the burdened load, but soon enough they pulled up in the city and parked their wagon in the busiest area they could find.

Once parked, they each held a skin up to the passing crowds and began shouting, "Hides for sale! Hides for sale! All of these hides for sale!"

The first man to approach their wagon was the local tanner who examined the goods and then spoke, "And how much are these hides you're selling, gentlemen?"

Hudden grinned at Dudden, then turned back to the tanner and answered, "Why, their weight in gold, sir!"

This made the man take a step back and looked the two over again. "It's a bit early to be stumbling from the tavern, isn't it?"

Shaking his head in disappointment for his wasted time, he hurried back to his tannery. Undeterred, the men kept shouting to the passing people about the hides they had up for sale. The second man to walk up was a cobbler, and he too began to examine the skins.

"How much are these being sold for, gentlemen?" he questioned the two.

This time it was Dudden who responded. "Why, their weight in gold, kind sir."

"I have no time for games!" the cobbler cried out. "Here is your deserved payment!"

He struck Hudden across the head with a blow that caused the farmer to stumble. As he staggered to the hide-filled wagon, the commotion had started to attract a larger crowd who began asking the cobbler what had happened, for he was a man of regard in the city.

"What has happened? Why have you struck him?" the crowd shouted.

"These scoundrels are trying to rip us all off by selling hides for their weight in gold!"

"Hold them!" bellowed the innkeeper from the crowd. "I'll bet they are with that other swindler who tricked me out of a year's worth of gold pieces, and all for a pathetic skin!"

Hearing the innkeepers allegations, the crowd fell on the two men, throwing punches and kicking hard until both Hudden and Dudden were chased from the town; bruised and hobbling.

All the way home, the two farmers spoke of nothing but Donald O'Neary and how, if they hated him before, they loathed him all the more now!

As it happened, Donald was journeying down the same path when he witnessed Hudden and Dudden limping in the distance. Noticing their torn clothes, blackened eyes, and bruised limbs, he shouted, "What ails you, my friends?" Followed by "What has happened? Perhaps some rogues met you on the road, or some thieves beset you on the return trip?"

"Don't speak compassion to us, you vagabond!" Dudden shouted, wincing from the movement. "I'll bet you think you're pretty clever, don't you? Sending us off with your merry lies? What have you got to say for yourself?"

"My friends," Donald began. "Who was lying to you? Didn't you see the gold on my table? Didn't you see me leaving with the skin and returning after without the skin?"

Yet despite all his reasonings, Hudden and Dudden were not swayed from their desire for revenge, and the two decided that Donald needed to pay!

They both acted quickly and fell upon O'Neary. While Hudden held him down, Dudden fetched a large sack from nearby. After a great deal of struggling, they forced Donald into the sack and promptly tied the end to allow him no hope of escaping.

Once the two men decided the knot was sufficient enough to keep him inside, they found a long, sturdy pole and strung the sack through it. Lifting it onto their shoulders, they set off down the path once more.

"And where am I being taken?" shouted Donald from within the sack.

Dudden gave the sack a swift kick before responding. "The Brown Lake isn't too far from here, and the bog there will do nicely."

Laughing with a pair of evil smiles, the two men carried Donald O'Neary off in the direction of Brown Lake. They walked for some time, but did not take into account how heavy the Donald-filled sack would be after a mile or two.

During one of their many rests on the side of the path, Hudden looked off into the distance and saw what looked to be a large inn. It had been quite some time since either man had truly rested, eaten a hearty meal, or drank a tasty beer, and considering the beating they had taken, the idea of sitting indoors for a brief moment was too good to pass up. With renewed vigor, they lifted the sack back up and did their best to hurry towards the inn.

"Dudden," said Hudden as they walked up to the front of the inn. "Let's set him down here for at least a spell because I am dead on my feet! We still have a ways to go and he is getting heavier by the step!"

Dudden nodded his approval to the plan, for his mouth was far too dry to speak. Of course, they didn't ask Donald for his opinion, and that is how O'Neary found himself dropped on the ground like a sack of potatoes.

"Hey, you!" Hudden gave the bag a swift kick. Donald grunted in response. "Stay here, sit still, and don't say nothin' to nobody! You're gonna wait here, not like you've much choice!"

The two men laughed as they plodded inside. Donald sat quietly for a while, but after some time had passed, he began to hear Hudden and Dudden's voices rise above the others in the inn. The raucous laughter and clinking of glasses let him know that the drinks were freely flowing.

Now, Donald O'Neary was very clever and while he sat bunched up in the sack, he engineered a plan to escape his situation and the two men inside. He shuffled and jumped about inside the bag to show that something alive was inside to anyone who might be nearby.

"I don't want her!" Donald began to say, just loud enough that it could be heard outside. "I tell you again, I will never want her! I will not have her!"

There was no response, so he tried again, but louder this time. "I won't have her! I don't want her!" Donald shouted over and over.

When still no one noticed he took in a deep breath and bellowed. **"I shall not have her! I do not want her!"**

It was the third time he shouted that he heard a voice answer back. "Just who is it you don't want and won't have?" It was a farmer who had come from a very long day in his fields and was looking forward to a brew inside. Behind the farmer stood his well-fed herd of cattle.

"The king's daughter," replied Donald to the farmer. "They tell me I must marry her, that I have no choice, but I *do not want her*!"

The farmer looked confused. "That doesn't seem like the dilemma you make it out to be, son. Seems you'd be lucky to be in that position!"

"Really?" Donald said as sarcastically as he possibly could. "Really? Do actually so?" There was almost a sneer to his voice. "So you're telling me that you think it would be an amazing feat to marry the daughter of a powerful king? To be dressed in gold and have treasures throughout life? That's what you're telling me?"

"Without a single doubt, yes!" answered the farmer, completely perplexed as to why this fool would want to pass up this chance. "Treasures, gold, and a princess, you say? You could take me along, you know?"

"Well," Donald said, then gave a long, dramatic pause, "I suppose you seem like an honest sort, and I would do anything to not wed the princess! Even though she is gorgeous and has rooms overflowing with jewels, she is not for me at all! Now, if you just let me out we can switch places, but from inside this sack I cannot escape on my own."

In a few quick motions, the farmer had the knots untied and in a few moments more the two men had switched places. Donald looked down into the sack before seeing to the knots.

"You must lie still as they take you to her; no matter the rocking, you mustn't move." Then Donald's mind came up with another idea. "Now, they will shout at you, call you names, and treat you like a vagrant, but it's all part of the act you must keep up if they believe you to be me. I must be crazy to give up this deal for you, though!"

The clever O'Neary acted as though he was reconsidering the deal. The farmer, not wanting to let this chance slip away, quickly responded, "No, no! You can take my cattle in trade, and you can escape this awful situation and let me be!"

He motioned towards the cows behind Donald. And off went Donald O'Neary down the path with the herd following close behind.

The night had become long when Hudden and Dudden finally emerged from the inn, swaying and trying to keep the other standing upright. Muttering and grumbling, they picked up the poles and started carrying the sack towards Brown Lake once again.

"Did he get heavier?" asked Hudden.

"Of course he feels heavier with how much you drank!" spat Dudden. "We're so close now."

The farmer decided to play his part to hurry the journey and began shouting, "I changed my mind, I want her now!" All it got him was another kick from the men.

"You'll have something, alright!" Hudden shouted, striking the sack with his fist.

"I want her now!" the farmer shouted, even louder now.

"No more tricks from you!" Dudden yelled as the two men heaved the sack into the lake with a mighty splash.

"You had this coming O'Neary!" Dudden bellowed as they turned and started back home.

Hudden and Dudden had a lighter step and happy smiles as they walked the familiar path back to their farms when they saw something in the distance. As they got closer, they realized that it was none other than Donald O'Neary standing next to a herd of healthy, happy cattle.

"No, it can't be you, Donald!" Dudden said in disbelief. "How did you escape and return back home faster than we did?"

"Well," Donald began with a grin, "I actually have you two to thank for my good fortune yet again. You may have had the wrong intent, but the result was quite good indeed! I mean, you *have* heard of the Land of Promise, right?"

Hudden and Dudden looked at each other and shrugged, neither ever having heard of such a place.

"As it so happens," Donald continued, "the Brown Lake leads right to this wondrous place, and as you can plainly see I stumbled across plenty!" He motioned to the cattle all around him grazing contentedly.

No matter how much they stared, neither Hudden nor Dudden could believe what was in front of them. Cattle; many fat, satisfied cattle.

"And that's not all," Donald said, patting a nearby cow. "These were the worst of what was down there."

"The worst?" Hudden asked incredulously.

"I couldn't get the others with me, they were all too fat. I mean, if I were them I wouldn't want to go either with all that bountiful grass stretching as far as you can see."

Hudden nudged Dudden, gave him a wink, and then looked back to Donald. "O'Neary, my fine fellow. I know we haven't always been on the best of terms, but I was just telling Dudden here about how much I respect you." Dudden nodded in agreement. "You'll show us how to get there, won't you? Won't you, my friend?"

"You are crazy if you think I would give anything down there to anyone besides myself," Donald answered, rolling his eyes. "There are more cattle than I have ever seen before, why would I do such a thing as show you the way?"

"It's true what they say, Dudden. The richer you get, the less you care. You weren't always this way, Donald, you were a nice guy before." expressed Hudden as he folded his arms. "Why keep all these blessings to yourself?"

"You two haven't been the kindest to me either, but you are right. I shall put aside the past for the sake of your futures! There are plenty of cattle and treasure for all of us, follow me!"

Donald comforted the cattle and left them to graze. As Donald led the way, Hudden and Dudden followed behind with greedy grins. The trip seemed faster this time, as they were walking towards prosperity as opposed to revenge.

When they reached the lake, Donald saw that the sky was filled with small puffs of white clouds and so the reflection on the Brown Lake mirrored them as though they were the same. With an outstretched hand and an excited tone, he hollered, "There! You can see them from here, men!" He pointed to the cloud's reflections dotting the surface.

"Where? Where are they?" shouted the two men, pushing and falling over each other to get to the water. Both dove deep into the lake, each wanting to be the first to find the cattle. Deeper and deeper they went, greedy smiles all the while.

Nothing was ever heard from either Hudden or Dudden ever again. As for Donald O'Neary, all his days were filled with joy and wealth, cattle and flock. His heart was full and so was his life until the end.

Chapter Two:

Master and Man

There was once a man with a one-track mind that only cared for the drink, and his name was Billy Mac Daniel. Not once did he turn a pint down, and he was never one to shy away from emptying a quart when necessary. His main concern was who would be paying for his drinks that night. He feared nothing but having naught to drink, and his joy was found in the amusement after he had downed many drinks. It was well known that if you began the night with Billy Mac Daniel, you'd end it throwing blows, for it was always with the greatest of ease that he fumbled his way into it.

If all that wasn't enough to pity the poor man, surely what would befall him next merits thinking sadly of him. For he was about to have a confrontation with some very bad company indeed; for they were the *good people* – fairies.

Only a few nights had passed since Christmas day and Billy Mac Daniel was taking his post-tavern stroll by the frost-covered fields. All his thoughts were on how fine a winter's night this was. Though, after some time walking, the nip in the air bit a little colder and he wished for a drink that seemed so far off.

"My, my, my," he said, breath hanging in the air like fog. "If only there was something that would bring some warmth to this man's soul, perhaps a drop of liquor – good liquor – would do the trick. Surely if this would happen, I would wish them the best I had ever wished a man!"

Billy jumped in fear when a small voice responded from behind him.

"You won't have to ask twice, Billy!"

There, standing as if the cold air meant nothing but a warm breeze, was a small, very well-dressed man. His hat was cut into three corners and sewn intricately with golden lace all around. Even his shoes were shined with large, silver buckles on their front that seemed so ornate and weighty that Billy wondered how this tiny figure managed to move at all.

Then Billy's attention caught what was in the tiny man's hand and nothing else mattered, for it was a thick, large glass nearly as big as the small man who held it. The aroma met Billy's nose and he could smell the quality of this liquor – better than he had ever smelled, and he knew it was top shelf, perhaps better than he had ever tasted.

"Very well met!" cheered Billy as he bent down and took the glass from the man's small hands.

Many men would have thought twice before accepting a gift from one of the *good people*, but his feelings towards the drink far surpassed his cautionary instinct. It was for this reason that Billy Mac Daniel found himself toasting the tiny man. "It matters not to me who is paying for the drink, I toast to your health and your generosity; you have my thanks!"

It was barely a breath before Billy had emptied the glass from top to bottom.

"Well met, indeed," agreed the small man, though his smile seemed more serious than before. "You are most welcome for the drink, Billy, but I am not like the other men who you trick and swindle for your drink; you will not cheat me as well! Now," he motioned in a hurried manner, "your purse. Out with your purse and pay me for your drink!"

At this, Billy did his best not to laugh, but he couldn't stifle it and the chuckle slipped through.

"Pay you? *You* are asking that I pay *you*?" He waved him off with one hand and wiped a laughing tear from his eye with the other. "Wouldn't it just be easier to scoop you up, put you in my pocket, and continue on as if you were nothing but a roadside berry?"

At this response, the small man's face became dark and heated; even the air seemed to spark with rage. "Billy Mac Daniel!" For such a tiny form, the voice was thunderous. "You had a chance, but now it is done! You shall be my servant for seven years and one day. Only then shall I consider myself fully repaid." Then, turning to depart, he said, "Now, follow me, Billy."

The instant the man became angry, Billy knew that he had made a grievous error in toying with one of the *good people*, but for some reason, he found himself unable to pull himself away. As the small man walked, so did Billy in step-by-step formation as though there was an invisible link between them.

Without a second's rest, the small man took Billy over hills and down into valleys, through rivers and fields, clearing bushes and hedges along the way; never braking, never stopping throughout the entire night.

When the glimmer of dawn began to creep over the horizon, the small man turned to Billy, "Off you go now, head on home. Rest. For tonight, you shall join me again without fail at the same field. You must not disappoint. If tonight you do not appear, it shall be a much worse thing for you indeed. However, if you behave yourself as an agreeable servant, you will find me to be a much more understanding master."

In a flash, the man was gone.

Billy listened to the words and took himself home. Despite being exhausted and wearier than he had ever been, sleep evaded him and every thought was of the punishment that would occur if he were to miss the meeting that night – or any other night after!

So much was his worry that he arose right at dusk and went to wait in that same field that he was instructed to without any hesitation. It wasn't long after nightfall when he heard rustling and the same voice spoke out from the grass, "Billy… Tonight your journey will be much longer than before, both of us shall traverse on horseback. Prepare one for yourself and saddle another for me. After the walk last night, I have no doubt that you are weary and the ride shall be of more ease."

The kindness took Billy off guard.

"My master," Billy asked, looking all around. "I only have a single question, for looking around as I am I see no stable or horses that are kept. I see a fort yonder, a twisted thorn tree by the field, a stream that runs at the bottom of the hill, and somewhat of a bog, but I see no horses."

"You are not to ask question, Billy," countered the small man. "Just listen. Go to the bog and pick two of the strongest reeds that are growing there and bring them to me."

Billy did as he was instructed, but all the while he wondered what intention the little man had in asking this of him. Doing as he was told, though, he found the strongest reeds, each with small blossoms growing to their sides, and he hurried them back to his master.

"Now you must get up, Billy," the little man said to him. As he said this, he took one of the reeds and sat upon it as though it was his steed. Billy leaned back in confusion.

"What am I getting up on, master?" For there was still no sight of a horse anywhere about, yet the small man was still straddling the reed.

"Get up on horseback, just as I am!" he retorted, irritated at the confusion to what he considered a very straightforward request.

"I see, you are out to make a fool of me," Billy said, examining the reed. "Asking me to get on horseback when it is merely a reed, one that I hand-picked, mind you! You expect me to believe this? Or maybe you will convince me that the reeds I pulled from your own bog are in fact horses to carry us away?" Billy got more sarcastic as he went on, each word further angering the small man.

"Not one more word! Up you get – UP!" roared the small man, fuming at this disrespect. "You are a fool if you think these are any different than the best horses you ever rode on!"

Billy thought that his master was trying to make a joke, and not wanting to anger him further, he did the same and straddled the reed himself. The little man immediately started yelling and kicking the air as though he was really riding a horse.

"Be great! Be great! Be great!" he cried out.

Not wanting to upset his master, Billy followed suit; yelling and kicking just as the little man was doing. Much to Billy's amazement, as they were both shouting, the reeds began to swell and transform until they became magnificent horses!

Without hesitation, the two steeds took off at a gallop with Billy and the little man riding them. Billy, however, had not given any thought to the style in which he sat on his reed and so he found himself facing the wrong direction as his horse sped off.

Even though he had ridden on many horses in his day, Billy had never been at this speed while facing the wrong way! Not having any time to think, he grabbed onto the first thing he could think of, which is how he ended up riding a horse while gripping its tail for dear life.

After a while, they pulled up in front of a massive gate, behind which was a sprawling estate with a very fine house at the center of the gardens and courtyards.

"Billy, hear me," his master whispered softly. "If I do something, you do it as well. You must follow me closely, but heed my words: because you gave no thought to the direction of your reed, thus not knowing your horse's head from its tail, be cautious this night. Keep your head about you and don't let yourself be turned about so that you don't know *your own* head from your tail."

Before he could answer, his master continued, "There may be drink ahead, and you must not get lost within it, for though it calls out in peace, liquor can make a man dumb!"

Raising his arms, the little man muttered some words which Billy could not understand, but as he said them, they both began to shrink until they were able to fit through the keyhole of the gate. From there they scurried to the next door and fit through that keyhole as well. The little man led them through door after door until they finally emerged in the wine cellar.

After the journey and subsequent experiences, seeing a room filled with all kinds of wine brought joy to Billy's heart. It wasn't a moment after they were in the room that the small man began drinking at a monstrous pace, and not wanting to be outdone, Billy followed suit with matching fervor.

In between drinks, Billy praised his master, "Surely, *surely* you must be the best master in all the world!" Then, after another drink, he said, "Even if I have many more masters after, none shall best you! If this is to be my payment, then I ask you never release me from your servitude!"

"That was not our bargain, and it shall not be changed to be so! Now up with you, follow me!" spat the little man, wiping his mouth of the wine.

Away they hurried, back through each keyhole until they found the horse-reeds which they left at the main gate. With wondrous speed, the two spoke the words, "Be great! Be great! Be great!"

The ground flew by as they galloped off, the dust kicked up like clouds behind them. When they slowed and returned to the field, the little man dismissed Billy for the night, repeating that he must be there the next night without fail.

And so the two went each night; Billy to the field, the little man meeting him, and then off on their steeds. Some nights they voyaged north, others took them far south until there was not a single wine cellar in all the land that they hadn't visited and drank from. It got to the point where Billy could tell the taste of the finest wines even better than the little man or the winemakers themselves!

One night when Billy arrived at the field ready to fetch the reeds from the bog for their horses, the little man stopped him and said, "Tonight we will need three reeds, for there will be a third horse. We may bring back more than we left with this night."

By now, Billy Mac Daniel knew better than to ask any questions about what he was told to do, so he went down to the bog and, as he had done before, selected the strongest reeds, making sure to bring back a third. He had no idea who this other member of their party was to be, nor why one would be needed. Was his master getting another servant?

"If he is out to find a second servant," said Billy as he made his way back to the field, "then it will be *he* who is made to go and fetch the reeds for the horses each night, for surely by now I have some standing with my master!"

But when he got to his master, nothing was said of it, and they set off for the night with Billy leading the third horse closely behind.

The two rode until they came to a cozy little farmhouse in the county of Limerick where everything lingered in the shadow of the monstrous Carrigogunnell Castle. It was the farmhouse however, that drew their attention due to the raucous noise coming from within.

The little man crept up to the door and, pressing his ear against it, took listen to all that was going on inside. After a while, he motioned for Billy to approach and whispered, "Billy, my servant, I will be one thousand years old tomorrow!" It was announced proudly and with a puffed chest.

"One thousand?" Billy asked, eyes wide and bewildered. "Will you really be that old, sir?"

At this, the little man grew red with anger and spat, "Never, ever doubt the words I say, boy!" Sputtering like a raging maniac, the little man continued his tirade. "If you dare to doubt me again, just once more, then you shall be ruined forever!"

Billy was taken aback at this outburst, but hung his head as he didn't want to further upset his master.

"Now, Billy," the little man said in a much calmer tone, smoothing his clothes from the tantrum. "As I will be turning one thousand years old tomorrow, it serves to reason that it is the perfect moment for me to marry!"

"Yes," Billy answered, nodding his head trying to keep up. "If you were to ever marry, it would make sense for this moment to be opportune."

"Precisely!" the little man clapped his hands, then turned his focus back to the farmhouse. "It is for that very reason that we are at *this* farmhouse on *this* night! Inside this very house, there is to be a wedding between the young Darbey Riley and the beautiful, tall Bridget Rooney. Now, seeing as she is a lovely girl that comes from a family in good standing, I feel that I should be the one to marry her. This night I shall take her off with us!"

As the little man finished explaining his plan, Billy stood quite unsure of this caper. "And what of Darbey Riley? What do you suppose he would have to say about this?"

"What did I say about questions, boy? I brought you here to assist, not to pester me with questions!" And so, not allowing Billy to squeeze another word in, he spoke the magical words again that shrunk them down, then through the keyhole and into the farmhouse they went.

Once inside, the mischievous pair saw the wedding congregation crowded in the hall. The little man climbed high into the rafters and, just like a small bird, perched and stalked those below. When Billy reached the same height, he sat slightly off-center with one leg dangling from the beam.

And so there they were, a fairy and Billy, watching from high above as the ceremony continued. As Billy looked on, he thought of Darbey and the cruel trick that his master was planning, which was made all the worse for how many of Billy's kin and loved ones seemed to be present.

The words carried clear into the rafters, and so as Billy and his master watched on, not a word went unheard. Darbey's father and two brothers were there, each with their sons. Close by were the proud parents of Bridget Rooney. To see their faces was to know that no two other people had ever held this much affection towards their daughter, and so they were right to, for Bridget was unlike the others.

More still, nearby were Bridget's four sisters, each with brand new dresses and accessories from head to toe, and also her three brothers dressed as clean and clever as they ever had been. The place was full; aunts, uncles, cousins – every table full, gossiping and happy. There was no lack of food or drink for anyone in the room, and the same could be said if the number had been doubled!

The feast was being prepared and, as tradition dictated, the bride and groom were to be first. And so, the priest instructed the roasted pig's head to be served. The new bride, excited in her role, went to help cut the pig's head and, in doing so, caused a burst of pepper to flutter into the air, causing her to give one giant sneeze.

Every guest and person in attendance looked up to offer a blessing, a "God bless you!", but they saw that the priest was by her side and thought that surely the priest would have blessed her immediately. However, the priest was preoccupied with the full table of food, and so he did not even notice the sneeze at all. And so the party continued without the sneeze being blessed by anyone!

Noticing this, the little man rocked with glee, his eyes twinkling with a most unkind light and his eyebrows became curved and malicious. "Ha, ha!" He laughed with a cruel tone, his hands wringing the other. "You see, now I have half of her! They let one sneeze pass, and all I need is for her to sneeze – unblessed – *twice more*, and then she shall be mine despite law, God, or priest!"

The little man leaned forward, eager to watch the night play out. Billy was not as happy at this result, seeing that he now understood his master's plan. Looking down from their perch, he cursed the thought of this little man stealing the bride away. What a terrible thing to do to such a pretty and young maid, only nineteen she was and a life full of possibility before her. Why did she deserve to be chained to such a wretched, twisted, unkind creature such as his master was? She had the bluest eyes and porcelain skin, while he was disfigured, ancient, and evil of spirit.

It must not be, he pondered.

She suddenly gave a second sneeze, but was shy and hid it from view so that a second unblessed sneeze went by. Billy was nervous and had no option that seemed best. If he were to do nothing, then surely this woman would be damned to live with his master forever, but if Billy spoke up, then he would bring the full weight of the little man's rage and power against him.

Suddenly, Billy heard a most unwelcome sound; the third sneeze from the bride. Without thinking, Billy rose to his legs and roared out, "God bless you!" He left it to echo throughout the room, cutting off his master's tie to the poor girl.

The explosion of rage from his master was a sight to behold; kicking and shouting, eyes flaming and skin red. When the little man finally spoke, his voice was a high shriek as though from a worn bagpipe. "Curses, curses! That's it, I discharge you forever from my care and give you *this* for all your payment!"

The little man gave a harsh and swift kick to Billy, sending him flying down from the height of the rafters. As Billy fell, he saw his master disappear in a furious puff of smoke right before Billy hit the main wedding table.

If the fall surprised Billy, imagine how the crowd below felt! Their shock was put to rest though, once Billy told them his tale of how he came to be there that night. Before long, the priest had heard the tale and immediately went about blessing the couple to ensure nothing befell either of them!

Billy Mac Daniel finished his evening by dancing many a merry dance. He didn't even realize that he hadn't had a drink, but his joy was none the less for it!

Chapter Three:

The Black Thief and the Knight of the Glen

In a time long past, there was once a king and queen who reigned over the south of Ireland. They had three beautiful sons, each one as radiant and charming as the next.

Times were good, until the queen suddenly fell dreadfully ill. It stole her strength and confined her to bed as she waited for death... Her sickness caused grief to cover the kingdom, and within the royal court, the sorrow was greater still. The king, her saddened husband, found no comfort in any of the words spoken to him by his advisors.

On one dark morning, she called the king before her as she felt death approaching quickly. Her hands were cold where warmth once was, and when he looked into her eyes they were pained and sad.

"My love," she said quietly, growing weaker by the moment. "The time has come for me to leave you, but even though I will be gone, you are still youthful and have years aplenty. You must, after my death, marry again, my dear." She continued despite the pained look on the king's face. "I have a request of you, though. Build a tower rising from the sea, and within that tower keep our three sons – those beautiful children – until they are of the age where they can act for themselves. I cannot bear the thought of another woman being a mother to my boys, so they shall be under no woman's power as they grow."

She coughed, voice growing fainter. "Ensure they get an education fitting their royal status, give them every opportunity from within their tower; train them as a king's son should be. I say this with all my heart, as it is all I have left to say. Farewell my lo…"

The king didn't even have a chance to answer her requests when her eyes closed to this world forever. He, with tears in his eyes, watched as she passed with a smile – her spirit released to the sky. The kingdom had never seen such mourning, and it was fitting for she was the best woman they had ever known. Be she rich or poor, the queen was better than them all in heart and action. This made the loss that much greater for the king, and he became inconsolable despite the attempts of the entire court. Mournful as he was, the king still adhered to what the queen had asked and it wasn't long before his three sons were ushered within the tower built on the sea.

The queen's words had been accurate, for in time the king's advisors guided him to not live a life in solitude, but instead to find a wife – another queen. Their counsel eventually won him over and the court chose the princess of their neighbor to the north, who was beautiful and wealthy, but struck no love in his heart. It was of no matter, for they were married in a swift fashion, which caused much joy and feasting around the kingdom.

Soon after this, the new queen gave birth to a fine new son, and this encouraged even more joy and feasting! It seemed as though with all the changes, even the memory of the old queen was slowly drifting away. And so it was that the king lived as happily as he could with his new queen.

One day, the queen had to go into the town to meet with the henwife. After their business was finished the queen went to leave, but stopped suddenly as she heard the henwife cry out, "If you return here again, I curse your neck to break in half!"

Confused and furious, the queen turned around and demanded to know why she was being spoken to in this demeaning manner. The old woman was known to be ornery and not of a pleasant nature, but this was an attack and an insult against royalty!

"Henwife! How dare you speak to your queen as such! Give me your reason immediately or it will be *your* neck that breaks!" the queen roared, her eyes aflame.

Without batting an eye the henwife responded, "I had to curse to this extent in order to get your attention! I have a very good reason that your life relies on you knowing, but to gain that knowledge from me you must pay dearly for it." She cackled.

"And what must I pay you, old woman? I must know this reason you speak of!"

"It is not so much to you, but a treasure to me," began the henwife. "I have a pack that I would need filled with wool, and I also have an old piece of pottery that must be filled with butter. More still, I have a barrel that I would need filled with wheat. All these things shall be your payment!"

This didn't seem the extravagant request it had originally begun as, so the queen relaxed herself and questioned, "This pack, how much wool will it take to fill?"

This caused the old woman to catch a glint in her eye. "That pack shall only be full with the wool from seven herds of sheep that have been sheared for seven years."

This made the queen gasp. "And the butter? How much is needed to fill this pottery of yours?"

"The output from seven dairy farms, oh queen, but it must be the sum of their output for seven years."

The queen seemed hesitant to question after the final form of payment, but she took a deep breath and asked, "Henwife, what of the wheat? How much shall satisfy your barrel?"

"The wheat that comes from seven fields, the sum over seven years, oh queen!"

Taking all this into account, the queen was defeated and decided to grant the henwife's demands. "You have asked for many things, and each in great quantity, but if what you say is true, then I must discover this reason you speak of. Thus, all you have asked for is yours."

Hearing this, the henwife nodded and stepped closer to the queen. "My reason for needing your attention is your stupidity!"

The queen was taken aback by this, but the old woman didn't give her a chance to respond and continued, "You cannot see beyond your own face to see the dangers that are looming over both you and your child! Grave danger is coming for you both!"

"Danger? I beg of you, tell me what you speak of! What endangers my child and I like this?" The queen fell to her knees, distraught at what she had heard.

"This danger lurks in a tower on the sea, built by your husband to carry out the final wishes of the first queen. She had him swear that their three sons would be kept there, away from a new queen's clutches and influence, until they are of age to return! So you see, if they are allowed to come of age and return, then the kingdom will surely be divided among them without thought to you or your child. You will be left desolate, alone, and without hope in this world."

As the henwife finished, the queen was weeping even more than before. She threw herself at the feet of the old woman.

"It shall take cunning and lies, but there is a way that you can keep what is rightfully yours." With the same nasty glint in her eye, the henwife continued, "You have to let the king know that you have discovered the truth about his three sons, but that he has nothing to fear from you. You must convince him to bring them back – all three sons. Tell him that you do not wish for them to be locked away any longer and that they must re-join the royal court once more.

"When the king hears this from you, he will be overcome with joy and a massive feast shall be arranged, along with plenty of festivities and entertainment for all to see and enjoy. Here is where you must play your part."

The queen listened closely, desperation clouding her judgment.

"You shall ask the three sons of the king to play a game of cards with you, and since you are the queen, you shall not be refused. When the bet is made, you must put forth a wager to the sons; if you win, then they must do whatever you so desire, but if they triumph, *you* shall do whatever they desire. Use no other cards but these." The queen was handed a pack of playing cards by the henwife. "As long as you play with none but these, you will almost certainly triumph."

Without hesitation, the queen clutched the cards from the old woman and thanked her for revealing all that she had. She hurried back to the palace where she rushed straight to the king, her mind set on the task before her. As nervous as she was, her voice stopped wavering once she began telling the king what she knew. The queen did all that the henwife instructed, telling the king that she knew of his sons and that he had nothing to fear from bringing them back to court. She played the part perfectly, and he saw nothing amiss about her request. In fact, he was overjoyed that she would desire for his sons to be back with him.

The entire place was filled with anticipation as they waited for the sons to return home, and once they did, they entered the kingdom with such fervor and glee at their unexpected release. As they were paraded through the streets, the queen noted that each son was indeed the picture of beauty and strength, quick in wit and charm, and of high intellect as well. It was easy to see why everyone was so drawn to them.

Rather than being like the others who had nothing but adoration for the sons, her jealousy was at full blaze by the time they were brought to the palace with the kingdom following in a jovial manner.

The party that followed spread from one end of the palace to the other and it was several hours before the queen found the chance to approach the three sons without a crowd interfering. Setting her voice sweetly, she greeted them.

"Dear princes," she said to the three, curtseying to the slightest degree. "I had hoped to find you alone, for I had hoped for you to join me in a game of cards. A wager always makes the evening that much more fun!"

She continued as a crowd gathered around them. The mass of people listened intently as the queen finished setting forth the terms of her proposal to the three princes. Not wanting to insult her, they all willingly agreed.

The oldest of the three sons sat at the table first and try as he may, the queen's bewitched deck delivered her the victory. The second eldest son did the same and lost, though not for lack of trying. The third son, the youngest, also sat down to play the queen, but this time he managed to outwit the henwife's deck and acquire the win for himself. This made the queen madder still, for he was the most handsome of the three and the one she wished control over the most.

The crowd around them were anxious to find out what sort of wish the queen would enact over the first two sons, thinking that this was all part of the celebration and that nothing devious would come of it. Using her clever mind, the queen concocted a task that seemed near to impossible, and even worse, she hid the true purpose from the two sons.

She told the crowd, "The two princes are to leave from here and go seek the Steed of Bells, belonging to the legendary Knight of the Glen."

If they failed in doing so, they would lose their heads upon returning. The crowd gasped in shock as they knew that no one had returned after leaving for such a quest.

The court quickly filled with whispers. Then the youngest prince who had been triumphant in his game spoke loudly and declared that his demand was ready for the queen.

Motioning to his brothers, he spoke to her, "My queen, you are sending my brothers off on a journey without knowledge of who or why they are searching. From what I have heard of these roads, the peril is great and without direction, they cannot have hope for success. Therefore, I request that they shall not depart alone, but rather I shall accompany them throughout this quest. I have knowledge that they seek the Steed, while you hid this from them, so I will be their guide."

The queen went to speak, but he cut her off with a swift motion. "That is not the extent of my desire. While we are on our journey, you shall stand atop the stronghold's highest point of the tallest tower and wait for either our return or news of our demise and failure. During this time you shall only eat cornmeal for food and tepid water for your drink! It shall be this way whether we are gone a day or seven years."

And with everything arranged, the queen climbed to the tower's peak and stood while the three princes set out on their quest.

The first thing that the youngest prince did once they navigated outside the kingdom walls was to reveal their true quest to his older brothers. He told them of the Steed, of the Knight, and how the queen expected them to fail and perish by not telling them all of the details. With renewed vigor, the three sons committed themselves to proving the queen wrong and returning triumphant.

The sons had not journeyed much further before they encountered a hobbled, elderly man struggling to make his way by the roadside. The three princes stopped and sat with the elderly man to rest, then set about partaking in conversation. The youngest prince noticed the striking black cap that this stranger wore, and so he inquired as to its significance and also who he was in name.

"The Thief of Sloan!" the old man said, doing his best to flourish while seated. "Though sometimes they call me the Black Thief." He tapped the cap on his head and winked. "Now where are you three off to, that you would take the time and aid an old man?"

The youngest saw the kindness in the man and trusted him enough to tell him the story of their lives from start to where they now sat. He spoke of the tower, of their now-passed mother, of the card game, and then of their current quest. The light was dimming as the prince finished his tale. "And that brings us to the here and now, where we are on the road, but have little idea of how to get to where we should be."

"My soul, what a tale!" said the Thief, shaking his head. "You are mighty brave little fellows, aren't you? Life is funny, ain't it? That same Steed that you are seeking is the very one that I myself have been hunting for seven years now. No one can even get near him because of the luxurious, silk covering that adorns him. It is covered in polished bells that echo through the air whenever he notices someone coming and begins to shake. The noise alerts the guards and everyone nearby to the attempted thievery going on. It is near impossible to get near, and even if you could lay a hand on him, the Knight of the Glen is always watching and will drag thieves to his fiery furnace where they are thrown and burnt into ashes."

The three princes were stunned into silence after hearing the full nature of their quest.

"My soul indeed," the youngest said, his eyes wide and his face pale. "How are we to return victorious? If we try to steal the Steed we will surely be caught, but if we return without it, we will lose our heads to the queen. Our fate is dark no matter which choice we make."

"I don't know about you three," the Thief started, "but in my eyes, there is more honor in dying at the hands of the Knight rather than the bitter queen. You aren't alone, anyways!" He threw his arms around the two eldest princes. "I will accompany you. I shall show you the way to the Glen, and whatever fortunes lay in store for us – life or death – I shall reap them with you!"

This touched the hearts of the princes, and they thanked him many times over for this brave deed. Had the sons set out on their own, it would have been eons before they could have found their way, but with the Black Thief in the lead, it wasn't long at all before they saw the castle rising in the distance.

"There she is, boys," the Thief said, shaking the dust from the road off his hat. "The Knight's castle. We will rest here until nightfall, for I know every inch of this land and our best chance for success is when darkness can shelter us. All the Knight keeps for watch after sunset is the bells of his Steed."

Some plans, no matter how well-prepared and considered, are doomed to fail from the start. For all their bravado and positivity, the Thief and the princes were setting themselves up to lose. They crept into the castle, made their way around the grounds to where the Steed slept. All of a sudden the mighty sound of bells filled the air as the beast began shaking itself in alarm. It was such a raucous sound that the Knight and every man of his were woken immediately and within moments had the four attempted thieves surrounded with no escape to be had.

Unceremoniously, they were hauled away up stairways, through hallways, and past rooms filled with effigies and ornaments, until they arrived deep within the Furnace Chamber where the Knight kept the flame burning for any thieves he may attract. From a distance, the captives felt the scorching heat and it only intensified as they were forced closer.

"Thieves!" bellowed a voice from above them, and the four prisoners looked up to see the Knight of the Glen overlooking the furnace. "You dared to try for my Steed, and here is the reward for your boldness! I have decided that yours should be a particularly horrible punishment, and so you shall be charred alive one by one!"

He gave a deep, booming laugh. "Stoke the flames, servants!" he shouted down to the men scurrying about the sides of the furnace. The Knight turned his attention back to the four hostages. "Start with the eldest of the three young ones! Then to the next youngest, and so on until the last to be burned is the man in the black cap there. His face looks like he has seen the most, and should watch the younger ones perish before him!"

"You guess correctly, sir!" spoke the Black Thief. "I have been near death many a time, but I have been even closer than the eldest prince here!" He pointed to the eldest of the sons who was being ushered forward by the Knight's servants.

"Hold!" the Knight said, holding his arm out towards the servants. He looked back to the Thief. "Closer than he? But he is mere strides from death! I say false, that you never were!"

"And yet it is true, and here I am alive to confirm it," the Thief said, adding his usual flourish.

"How could that be? Death so near and yet you still live? This I must hear." Upon hearing this, the Thief of Sloan knew that he had his chance to concoct an escape plan of sorts. The Knight came down to where they were standing to hear the Thief's account more clearly.

"Now, Sir," said the Thief, leaning in towards the Knight. "If you believe that the danger I escaped was far more dire than this young man's, will you let him free?" he queried, pointing to the eldest of the princes.

"If you were truly that close to death and survived, I shall agree and release him from his bindings. Now, your story." The Knight motioned for the Thief to continue, and so he did.

"When I was a young boy I was much wilder than I am now, and because of that, I found trouble far too often. During one of my nomadic times, I found myself without any lodging. As night began to fall, I came across a barn and I climbed up into the rafters and hid myself for slumber. I had barely put my head down when I heard voices below. It was three witches who had each come into the barn carrying a bag full of gold!

"One by one, they laid on the ground, placing the bags under their heads to use as pillows. One witch turned to the other and whispered, 'Now our gold shall be safe,' They nodded in agreeance and after some time the three witches fell fast asleep.

"I crept down to the ground and saw large tufts of grass and sod piles along the side of the barn. I tip-toed to each witch and carefully switched their sacks of gold with a chunk of turf. And within a flash I hurried off from the barn, lest I be found and caught!

"Alas, it wasn't a minute before I saw three beasts in pursuit; a hare, a hound, and a hawk! I knew it to be the three witches in animal form to ensure that I couldn't escape by land or by sea with one to stalk me from the air. However, none of their forms were of intimidation to me. I was determined to defend myself and escape with the gold, but if they had the power to shift shape, what use would my sword be against them? Perhaps they could return from death!

"I decided that rather than violence, I would find a tree and hide within the thickness of the branches. The effort was of considerable difficulty with a sword and bags of gold in tow, but I climbed my way further up until I felt as though I was a safe distance away.

"This did not deter the witches though, and once they discovered my whereabouts they shifted yet again; this time into a blacksmith's anvil, a bull-sized man, and a scrap of iron. It didn't take long for the witches to forge the iron into an axe, and the large man set about hacking down the tree. I had no place to run, so I was stuck there as the axe dug deeper into the bark.

"Soon the tree began to give more to each strike and I knew that it would only take a few more to collapse the entire thing, sending me to my death. I was counting down the seconds until the final blow would hit when suddenly the cry of a rooster rang through the air signaling the rise of a new day.

"With awful sounds, the witches morphed back into their natural forms and left immediately for fear of being seen for what they were. I waited for some time before sliding down the wonky tree with my sword, my gold, and my life intact!"

"Now, sir," the Thief said to the Knight. "If being a single axe strike from death isn't the story you hoped for, I leave it for you to decide."

"That is the most fantastic thing I have ever heard!" the Knight answered, truly shocked. He waved towards his servants. "My word was given, this eldest one shall go free. Sadly, the next one shall be burned now and nothing can be done."

The Thief tapped his foot on the floor and spoke. "Indeed, indeed. However," he said, drawing the Knight's attention once more, "I do not think this one will burn either."

"And why is that, Thief?" the Knight balked.

"Simply because I have escaped death even closer still than the witches I spoke of! If I speak true, this man is free as well."

"A danger as great as the first? Impossible, so I agree again to your terms," said the Knight.

"I said I lived wild, and that kind of life runs out of gold quite quickly. My options had run dry and I was without hope when I heard that a local priest had passed away. So beloved was he that his burial shroud was weaved in gold and covered in jewels. I saw this as an opportunity for riches and resolved to take all the treasures I could carry.

"I tiptoed inside the long, ghoulish vault where the priest was laid to rest, and within an instant I heard footsteps scurrying towards me. My first thought was that the spirit of the priest had come to protect the grave, so I hid myself away.

"I peeked out from cover and saw a large silhouette of a man blocking the doorway. In fear of being caught I rushed in to immobilize the intimidating figure with a swift blow. Seeing the mortal reaction, I recognized that it was not the protective spirit I initially thought was out to get me, and I turned and ventured deeper into the vault.

"Reaching the end of the hall, I found where the priest was laid to rest. Rifling through the robes of the corpse, I discovered that someone had been there before me. This is when it struck me. The figure at the doorway must have been a graverobber that beat me to all the riches.

"I hurried back to the entrance, where the robber lay limp, but stopped when I saw guards hurrying towards the vault. Ducking down out of sight, I heard one of them shout, 'Check the vault! Surely no one would stoop low enough to rob a corpse!'

"I was filled with fear, if they saw me then I would surely be killed, but I needed to escape, so I concocted a plan.

"Lifting the dead thief at the doorway, I made him move as though alive, immediately causing the guards to attack the decoy. The guards felt emboldened and rushed into the vault right past where I was hidden. With a deep breath, I hurried out and escaped, ensuring they would never get their hands on the Black Thief."

"Well then," the Knight said slowly, his eyes wide still. "You have proved your story amusing for a second time, and for a second time my word is my word." He turned to the servants holding the second-eldest. "He is to be released, but there is still the third son that will be burned, and no person could have a third story about evading death's grasp. It's a pity that today this boy dies."

The servants let the second son go, and gripped the youngest prince tight, turning him towards the furnace.

"As it turns out, this boy is my favorite," chuckled the Thief. "Wouldn't you know that, for a third time, I brushed the cloak of death and escaped? Likewise, for a third time, you will set the boy free if I speak true."

The Knight nodded in agreement, looking skeptically at the Thief.

"My travels have taken me the world over, but on this occasion, I happened across a large, thick forest which I could not find my way out from. After trudging through the woods for some time, I came across a gigantic castle! I was exhausted and needed shelter, so I crept through the gate and into the courtyard where I found a young woman in tears, and a young child sitting on her knee.

" 'My dear,' I asked, for it was clear she felt pain. 'What has made you cry like this? And who is the lord of this place?' For other than the woman, I had seen hint of no one else.

" 'It is good that you have not met him, nor shall you for he is not here now. A monstrous one, he is! A single eye on his face and an insatiable craving for human flesh.' She held up the child who was with her. 'He brought me this child and bid me make it into a pie for him! That command is enough to break anyone's spirit.'

"I knew that I had to help this woman, and so I asked if she knew anywhere that I could hide the child so that this horrible beast would not eat it. The woman told me of a house a good distance away where an elderly widow would care for it, but there was a question she had for me.

" 'What of this pie I am supposed to make from the child? Won't the lord know?' But I, being the Thief of Sloan, had a plan in mind.

" 'I shall go off into the forest and kill a wild pig for its meat, and you shall take the child's hand and slice off one finger. Once the pie is prepared we will stick the finger in so that it is noticeable, thus fooling this beast of a man!'

"It was risky, but it was our only option before he returned. So the woman severed the child's finger and I took the child off to the widow's abode to be kept safe while the woman cooked the wild pig. Moments after returning back to the woman, we were startled by the sounds of the monstrous lord riding in.

" 'Bless me, he has returned much sooner than I thought!' cried the woman. 'We must hide you away or else we will all perish! There is a chamber where all the bodies from his victims are stored, and we can hide you in there! Strip down as the others are, and he will be none the wiser.' I did as she asked and soon I was well-hidden among the bodies.

"When the woman set the pie before her master, he inhaled a deep breath and remarked how the pie smelt alike to wild pig, but the woman was alert and crafty. She immediately turned his attention to the finger, and seeing evidence of the child, he was content with the pie and inhaled it in just a few gulps. This did not satiate him however, for no sooner had he eaten the entire pie was he asking for more.

"Rubbing his belly, the beast set off for the chamber of corpses where I was carefully hidden away! I could not move or speak despite his huge hand groping all about me, and finally, he gripped my leg with a strength I'd never felt before! And with a painful slice, he cut skin from my hip and took the flesh to be roasted. I did not cry out, though it was agonizing, any sound would have certainly meant my death!

"He ate and ate, then drank and drank. Before long, it all went to his head and the beast passed out. I heard his loud snoring and decided it to be my last chance to hurriedly sneak over to the woman to tend to my wound. Not long after, I crept toward the fire and lifted the iron spit from atop the flames. Then, using all of my might, I plunged it deep into the one eye of this horrifying beast! Despite the reddened metal and roar of pain, the lord of the castle did not succumb to this strike. His bellows curdled the blood and he swept his arms all about in a blind rage.

"In a panic, I ran from the castle and nearly considered myself free until I heard the booming steps of the one-eyed beast roaring behind me. The spit still penetrating through his skull, blind and bloody, he cried out as he lumbered after me.

"I knew myself to be faster than he, and the injury would surely slow him down, but I did not know of the enchanted ring he kept for drastic moments such as this one! When the giant called out, the ring answered back so that neither were ever unaware of their locations. With great aim, the beast heaved this ring toward me and it latched itself to my toe, catching me off guard.

"There was nowhere to run and nowhere to hide because the ring called its master stridently and frequently. I had no option, drew my dagger from its sheath – one swipe removed the toe and the ring with it. As quickly as I could, I threw the toe with the ring still attached into a deep lake nearby and then kept running towards escape, toe or no toe! The beast, still trailing the calls from the ring, dove into the deep waters and drowned at the bottom!

"So you see, Knight of the Glen, you have heard the dangers that I have escaped from. Indeed, more proof is the limp I suffer with from my missing toe." When the Thief finished the story, an old woman who had been silent in the corner stepped forward and rested her hand on the Knight's shoulder.

"This man, this Thief, speaks truthfully, oh Knight," she said, her voice hoarse and cracked.

"How do you know this, woman?" the Knight responded with skepticism.

"That woman who the Thief encountered in the castle? It was me! And the child she begged him to rescue? That was you, dear Knight! This Thief before you is the reason you were not cooked and eaten by that atrocious beast! Though your finger may be lost, your life was spared."

"Oh my." The Knight was completely overwhelmed by what he had heard. "Are you and my rescuer one in the same, Black Thief? You are why I live?"

The Thief nodded, his head bowed.

"What joy this is then!" the Knight exclaimed, cheer filling every part of the air about him. "Not only shall all of you be pardoned, but never again shall you want for anything! You shall live without need in my castle, and retire on my lands for the rest of your lives!"

"As gracious as you are, oh Knight," said the Thief. "We are here on a mission."

He told the Knight all about the queen and her deceit, then their perils up until that moment. The Thief said that they could not leave without the Steed, lest the queen found out and have the three sons executed.

"Then you shall have my Steed!" the Knight heartily agreed. "Better that than this fellow lose his life. But please return and visit on occasion as I would love to learn more about my savior and the many stories you may have to tell."

And with the promise to return agreed, the sons and the Black Thief departed for their journey home.

All the while they had been gone from their home, the queen had been standing atop the tower as she was commanded. On one morning she saw figures approaching from the distance and the instant she heard the ringing bells from the Steed's cover she knew that she had been bested. With a mournful cry, she threw herself from the heights of the tower and shattered her body on the rocks below.

The kingdom took no loss from the queen's death, for the three sons lived happily during their father's reign and for long after that.

Chapter Four:

The Fairy Nurse

In the small town of Coolgarrow there lived a farmer and his wife. The lovely couple had three children, one of which was just an infant. The farmer's wife was a good wife, but there were many who thought she was not as dedicated to her family as she should be. In truth, she loved her family, but any time spent praying or in church had always seemed too time-consuming and tedious for her. When she did fall to her knees at night to pray, more often than not the farmer found his wife sound asleep without concluding her prayers.

On the farm there had been distress amongst the animals, and there was word of a fairy man that could be of some help. One day, instead of attending church with her spouse and children, she opted to meet with this fairy man in concern for her livestock.

This meeting took much longer than she anticipated and when she finally did arrive at church, every one gave her quite the stare! The rest of the day she was sincerely apologetic, for she knew her husband was feeling shame for her actions and she loved him dearly.

Later that very same night the farmer was awakened by awful screams coming from his children's room. "Mother! Mother!" they cried out.

He turned over and found that his wife was no longer beside him. He went to the bedside of his children and asked them what happened to their mother and why they were crying for her.

The eldest child, fear in his eyes, said that he had seen his mother surrounded by small, well-dressed people who escorted her outside and into the night. Try as they did, however, they could find no trace of her or the little people who were supposedly with her.

Many days passed without anyone hearing a word of her whereabouts. With her gone, it had been a troubled time. The children were minded by a neighbor where possible, while the infant was cared for by a nurse. And still, nothing was heard from the farmer's wife.

A month and a half after her disappearance, the farmer was leaving for the fields early one morning when a neighborly woman grabbed his attention by the roadside. She had a grim look about her as she began to tell him a most disturbing tale.

"Last night right before I fell asleep, a horse's whinny from outside stirred me from my bed. A knock at the door brought me to find a tall, dark man on a large horse who beckoned me to follow him. He said that there was a lady who had a great need of my skills and that we had to make haste. I threw on my cloak and barely had time to close the door before he had whisked me up onto the horse behind him.

"Where is this lady who demands my presence?" I asked him.

"You will know before long," he answered. Then he drew his fingers across my eyes, and all light was snuffed out. I couldn't see a single thing for the entire journey and could only hold tight in hopes that he didn't let me fall. After hours of riding, I felt a jostle and he lifted me down and set my feet on the firm ground, for which I was most grateful. He drew his fingers the other way across my eyes and the world was reopened to me.

"In front of me was a massive castle with ornate doors rising high into the fortifications. He took me through the gate and into a great hall where fine colors swirled about the room. Gold and silver ornaments, the finest furniture and rugs, lush carpets stretching further than I could see; it was a sight to behold. From the windows, I could see green hills through the thin, fine curtains.

"After walking about for some time, he led me to a bedroom where a beautiful woman sat, dressed in the prettiest white dress. Beside her was a healthy, smiling baby boy, reaching about as children do. She acknowledged me and then clapped, which motioned the man to go over to her and kiss her and the child. He turned and handed me a bottle of ointment and praised me for coming with him, then asked for me to put the ointment all over the child.

"I had been given no reason to deny their request, and I was brought to aid, so I did as they asked and began rubbing the ointment all over the baby. After a minute, my eye began to sting and so, without thinking, I rubbed it with an ointment-covered finger and when I looked back up the sight that I beheld was awful and hideous indeed!

"Where there had been beauty and fine things was now a dreary, moldy cave with stale waters seeping throughout the cracks and walls. But the worst still was what the people had become.

"The woman and man were now hobbled, emaciated, and twisted in distorted ways. The child was nothing but skin and bone, unsmiling and pale. Their breath was wheezy and all about me the air was stagnant and thick. I caught my breath and made sure to not show my fear at what had been revealed. After a while, the man told me to go to the hall and wait for him to see me safely home.

"Standing by the door to the room was your wife, Molly, looking as scared as I was. She hurried over to me and in a soft whisper said that she had been brought by the same dark man to be the nursemaid to the children of the fairy kings and queens.

" 'I have been here without hope of escape,' Molly said. 'That is, until now that I see you here. I have an idea in how I can be released from my capture here, but my husband must be as committed as I. You see, next Friday night the fairy procession shall pass by the town where our farm is built and kept. When we pass by the road, he must leap up and grab onto me without dreaming of letting go. The fairies will do all manner of things to keep me, but he must not let go!'

"She told me that you would need to muster all of your courage, but that if you didn't lose your grip, she would be safe. Then, your wife saw the dark man approaching and whispered once more to me. 'Here is the king, so I must go. Do not respond, and don't let them know about the ointment.

"The man didn't even give Molly a second thought when he returned to lead me home. He had me follow him out of the castle that I knew to be a cave, and when we emerged I saw the place for what it truly was. No green grass or health sprouted, only dirty water and sickness. Even the horse we had ridden was not the fine steed I had first seen, but a sickly, weak beast that I was amazed could even stand at all.

"I was racked with fear the entire ride home, but finally, the fairy king had me back at my home where he helped me from the awful horse and handed me a sack in which he said were five gold coins. Thanking me, he turned and rode off into the night, leaving me alone. I fell to my knees as the fear hit me full force and frightened tears flowed freely. When I finally made it to my bed, I could not sleep for all I saw were the night's horrors in my mind.

"This morning I checked the sack of gold coins and found nothing but soggy leaves! Another trick by the fairies. Knowing all that I have told you, what are you to do?" She ended her story and looked to see how the farmer would react.

Standing shocked in what he had just heard, the farmer resolved in his courage proclaimed "We must wait by the roadside on Friday to free my wife from the fairies!" The two concluded their discussions and agreed to meet again on Friday to rescue poor Molly.

On that Friday the pair met again and prepared for where the fairies were supposed to be passing by. Looking down the road in either direction, the farmer could see not a person, let alone a procession of fairies. This is why he was so surprised when the woman beside him began frantically shaking his arm and pointing.

"They are here! I see them in the distance! Surely you can hear them now; the jingling bells and laughter from the party?"

But the farmer still saw an empty road despite everything the woman said. He realized then and there that because of the ointment, the woman could now see into the fairy realm but he could not!

"Alas! How am I to catch my wife and wrench her from the fairies if I cannot even see what I am aiming for? I will be made the fool and jump at nothing, leaving me to be alone and her to remain with them forever!" he cried mournfully, tears falling to the dirt.

The woman stepped up and spoke firmly. "It will not be so! You may not see them, but *I do*! I shall be the one who looks and when your wife is directly before you I will push you from behind and it is then that this plan lies with you! For if you don't use all your courage and bravery, all your strength and cunning, she will be gone forever!"

And so, the farmer poised himself at the edge of the road with the woman behind him, ready to push at the moment of action.

It was a tense time that seemed to stretch on forever, but soon enough the woman said, "I see her, I see your wife approaching. Remember, it will be your sorrow if you fail to act!"

Before another moment passed, he felt the woman give him a shove and he called upon everything within him when he leaped through the air, arms outstretched. For a brief second, he feared that he had missed his intended target, but all of a sudden he felt something enter his arms and suddenly his eyes were truly opened. He saw his arms gripping the waist of his wife atop the dark horse of the fairy king.

A smile began to widen on his face, but within an instant the farmer was bombarded with jeers and vicious roars surrounded by horrible-looking creatures. The fairies had noticed him and were not about to let their nursemaid go without a fight!

Back and forth they jostled, but nothing could weaken the farmers grip on his wife's waist, not even a horde of fairies with malice on their minds. Like winged locusts, they fluttered about and their typically peaceful faces became distorted and cruel in appearance.

Bidding them begone in God's name, the farmer shouted in rebuttal as he continued to hold on for dear life. While still holding on tightly, he shaped his hands together in the form of a cross. And in a flash, the noise and procession vanished. All that remained was Molly lying in the arms of her husband and the older woman smiling as she looked on from the roadside. The plan worked! Happiness suddenly filled the air in amazement at all that had happened. In good time the family lived on together with laughter and love. Although, after her fright, Molly spent more time on her knees and never thought to seek assistance from the fairies ever again.

Chapter Five:

The Believing Husbands

In the land of Erin, quite some time ago, there resided a young man. Now, this particular lad was seeking a wife. During his search, he discovered that he fostered a love for only one woman; the only daughter of a local farmer. He approached the farmer for his blessing, and it was given. Next, he went to the girl and asked for her hand in marriage, and she graciously accepted. And in no time the couple had settled down on a homely farm of their own.

The two lovebirds tended to their land and grew fonder with each passing day. Every year there came a time when they needed to harvest the moss from around the farm and lay it out to dry, thus giving them fuel for the winter fires. On one very fine day during that season, the husband and wife set out to their tasks, accompanied by the wife's mother and father. They journeyed to the moors and after hours of demanding work, their hunger began to take over.

"Hurry home and fetch us all a feast my beloved, but remember we have been gone for quite some time and the horses will be hungry as well," yelled the farmer across the moor.

"Do not fret, I will tend to the horses before I return," she replied as she turned to make her way back to the farm.

The journey back was a tiresome one and by the time she arrived at the stables, she was exhausted. Without paying much attention, she made her way through the open doors and gasped aloud when she saw a gigantic, heavy-laden saddle pack belonging to their strongest, speckled mare dangling high above her. It seemed to loom over her and in her fright she gave a leap and a scream.

"Oh!" Her hand clasped to her heaving chest. "How dreadful it would have been to be crushed by such a monstrous saddle pack! It certainly would have killed me, and my husband far off in the moors!" She was so overtaken by the moment that she dropped down right there in the stables and burst into hysterical tears.

The farmer noticed how much time had gone by since his wife left to prepare their dinner, and he turned to his father and mother-in-law with concern.

"It's been hours, where has she gone off to?" he asked, hands on his hips.

Her father had no answer while her mother began to worry more and more. It wasn't long before she refused to work any longer and demanded they let her return to the farm and check on her daughter.

When the men finally conceded, the mother hurried across the moor, through the fields, and finally arrived back at the farm. Look as she might all about the house, her daughter could not be found. Evidentially the same in the dairy and shed, which by now had caused the worried mother to weep. Through her tears she made her way to the stable where she found her daughter, face in her hands, crying loudly on the floor.

"My dear!" her mother shouted. "What could be *this* wrong that you never returned to us?"

Raising her head, still sobbing, she answered between staggered breaths.

"I went to f-f-feed the horses, m-m-mother," she stammered through the tears, her voice cracking and wavering. "Then I s-s-saw the saddle pack! High above my head and it could've k-k-killed me! Fallen r-r-right on me, crushing me to death!"

By the time she finished, her crying had reached the loudest volume yet.

Raising her hands to the heavens, the girl's mother cried out as well. "What a terrible thing it would have been!" Her voice also began to crack as the tears streamed down her face. "What would I ever do if you were killed? I would never make it!"

The tears overwhelmed her and she fell to the floor right beside her daughter and the two of them wept up a woeful storm.

Back on the moor, the farmer and his father-in-law were growing increasingly concerned considering how long it had been since either of the wives had returned.

"Whatever has happened must be dreadful indeed for it to stop them both from returning back to us," said the farmer's father-in-law. "Enough time has passed, I need to go check on them. I cannot wait any longer!"

The father-in-law nodded to the farmer, and away he went; over the moor, through the fields, and reaching the farm as fast as he could.

Just as the mother had done, he searched the house, the dairy, and the shed before turning his sights towards the stables. Right before he entered the building, he heard the cacophony of sobbing that was going on inside. Racing the last few steps he found both women on the floor in hysterics.

"What could be *this* wrong?" he exclaimed, eyes wide and heart thumping.

"It's awful!" cried the mother. "Horrible! Your daughter came into the stables to feed the horses and when she looked up she saw the mare's saddle pack, heavy and terrifying, and it overwhelmed her to think of what would have happened if it fell onto her, killing her!" She finished speaking only to continue her sobbing.

"How horrible!" he exclaimed, his hands over his face as he collapsed into tears. "My only daughter would have been taken from me!"

And there the three of them were; sobbing on the floor of the stables.

It was night before the young farmer made his way back from the moors, his day's work complete and filled with thoughts of worry regarding his family; none of which had returned. He was hungry and tired as he searched through the house, but it was empty.

He rummaged around the farm until finally he heard the cries of his wife and her parents in the stables. In a hurry, he burst in and saw them all sobbing on the floor.

"Why are you all here? What has happened today to keep all of you away for this long?" he asked breathlessly.

"Your wife nearly died!" the father cried out, his hands trembling. "She came into the stable, to feed the horses, and when she saw that heavy saddle pack way up there, she was overcome by the thought of it falling and striking her dead!"

"How awful!" the three on the floor sobbed together.

The farmer, however, seemed to be unaffected. "It didn't fall, and it didn't kill her though."

The young man walked back to the house to fill his belly. The three were left in the stables to cry until they could cry no more.

After the night had passed, the farmer rose and called the family together at the kitchen table. "My wife, the parents of my beloved, I am setting off today; leaving this house."

This sent the three at the table into a fit of perplexity.

"Family!" the farmer continued, shouting over them. "I shall not return to this house until I have found three people sillier than you lot!"

And despite their disagreement, he packed and left that very day.

It was not long before he stumbled across a small town. The first home to come into vision was a quaint cottage with its doors wide open, seeming to beckon him in. Cautiously entering, he found three old women sitting at spinning wheels. All three looked up the moment he walked in and gazed at the young man standing at the doorway. Something seemed off, a strange feeling lingered about within him.

"You three don't belong here in this town, do you?" he asked.

"We are from far off, but then again, you aren't from here either, are you?" the old women answered in unison.

"You speak with precision, but riddle me this: is this town a good place to live?" the farmer replied to them.

After the women all exchanged long looks, they turned to him and responded.

"We enjoy it quite a bit, actually!" they said gleefully, cackling. "The men of this town are the silliest we have *ever* encountered, and because of that, we can make them believe anything at all! In fact, we already have three of them believing that we are their wives!"

This struck the ears of the farmer as a great potential spot to pursue his quest to find the silliest folks. He reached deep into his cloak and pulled out a solid gold ring.

"This ring can be yours," he said, holding it up to them. "But it will only be gifted to the woman who makes her spouse believe something truly and completely impossible."

With a loud cry, the three women agreed to this task and each one returned to the home of the men they had tricked.

"Oh, my husband!" said the first woman. "You are so sick!" she exclaimed, holding him close.

"Sick? Am I sick, wife?" he asked, looking puzzled and concerned.

"Oh, yes!" she replied. "You must immediately take off your clothes and lie down! Right away!"

She hurried him towards the bed. When he had disrobed and was in bed, she looked at him and declared, "Husband, how awful! You are dead!"

"Dead? Really?" he asked, even more nervous.

"Very much so, husband. Rather dead. Unable to move either hand or foot, eyes or mouth!" the woman cried out.

As the silly man he was, he believed her every word and acted fully as though he was dead, for to him he was.

The second man returned home to find his 'wife' also waiting for his arrival.

"Who are you? You are not my husband? You are not yourself!" she shouted as he walked in the door, shielding her face with her hands.

"I am not myself?" he asked, his eyes open wide.

"No, not at all. You are not yourself," his 'wife' answered him, and lacking an identity, he wandered off into the middle of the woods.

The third man came home and entered to find his 'wife' preparing dinner. They ate together and without any event, the night passed; both sleeping soundly. When morning came, the man heard a knocking at the door. Upon opening it, he found a small boy there with a message that there was to be a funeral of a man he knew. He rushed back to bed and woke his 'wife' with news of the funeral.

"I must depart and attend the funeral," he told her.

"There is still plenty of time," she whispered to him, setting him back down in bed. It wasn't long before they heard the sounds of the funeral procession outside the window in the distance.

"Husband, rise and hurry up!" the woman shouted, shaking the man from his bed. In a panic he jumped out of bed and looked around for his clothes. "Hurry, husband, be off!"

"I have no clothes, wife!" he yelled back, still confused and in a state.

"My silly husband, you are dressed already! You are wearing your clothes," she said plainly, as though it was the most truthful thing ever.

He turned all about, looking at himself. "I am dressed?"

"You are."

"I have clothes on my body?"

"You do. Now make haste or else they'll have buried him long before you even get there!"

Like the swiftest wind, the man ran through the streets without pause until he finally came upon the procession. Instead of the welcome he expected, the mourners yelled and shouted as they pushed to get away from him, for they saw a naked, crazed man tearing towards them.

After a few moments of silence, a man emerged from the nearby woods and seeing the naked man standing next to the coffin he asked a question.

"Do you know who I am?" the man who had just come from the woods asked.

"I don't believe so, sir," answered the naked man. "I'm quite sure I don't know you."

"So why are you naked?"

"Naked? No, no, sir. My wife assured me that I had clothes on before I left to catch this funeral."

"My wife said I was dead!" shouted the voice inside the coffin.

The instant the two men heard the voice inside the coffin, they squealed in fear and hurried back to their own homes. Still confused, the third man climbed out of the coffin and returned home to find his 'wife' seated at the table, caressing a spangled golden ring, for he had been the silliest.

As for the young farmer, he set off on his return journey with his quest fulfilled and proof of more silliness than he had at home.

Chapter Six:

Connla and the Fairy Maiden

On the hill known as *Usna* stood a king, Conn of the Hundred Fights, and his son, Connla of the Fiery Hair. While the two looked down from the highest point of *Usna*, Connla saw a young woman approaching garbed in strange clothing.

"Where have you come from?" asked Connla.

"I have come from the Plains of the Ever Living," answered the maiden. "There is no sin, there is no death; we are joyful always, and that joy never ceases nor grows weary. Nothing takes away from our pleasure; trouble cannot find us. The men call us Hill Folk because we have made our homes deep in the round, green hills of the Plains."

While the maiden was speaking, the king stood perplexed because even though he could plainly hear the voice of the woman, there was no physical being present. The kings men all looked around in confusion as well, for they too only heard the voice and could see no woman. Connla was the only one of them that was able to see the maiden's form.

"To who are you speaking to, my son?" asked Conn, the king.

The woman responded instead. "Your son, Connla, speaks to a young, beautiful woman who never ages and shall never die. I love your son, and I have come to call him away to the *Moy Mell*, the Plain of Pleasure. There, Boadag is king, and during his reign, there has been no complaint nor sorrow in all the land."

She turned her eyes and voice towards Connla. "Come away with me, oh, Connla of the Fiery Hair; skin as ruddy as the dawn and tawny. A fairy crown is waiting to be set upon those handsome features, your wondrous face, and royal form."

She smiled, beautiful and bewitching. "Come! Come, and your youth shall never fade, nor your handsomeness be lost to time, nor till the judgment comes on the last day!"

Everything the king heard made him fearful and so he called out loudly for his druid, Coran, to stand at his side. The druid hurried forward, and the king spoke.

"Oh, Coran of many spells! You wield cunning magic, I call upon you to aid me with it," he said to the druid. "The task before me is far too great for even *my* skill, wit, or ability. Not in my time as king has something so great presented itself!"

The king, trouble growing, continued, "A woman – an unseen, invisible maiden – has met us, and by some horrible power wants to tear my dearest, handsome son from me. If you do not help me then he will be taken from this king – *your* king – by this woman's treachery, magic, and wiles!"

Coran the druid charged forward and began chanting his incantations towards where he had previously heard the woman's voice. After the druid casted his spells, the voice lulled into silence, nor did Connla see the maiden before him any longer.

Right before she vanished, the woman tossed an apple to Connla.

For an entire month since that day Connla would neither eat nor drink unless it be from the enchanted apple he had been bestowed. Upon each mouthful, the apple magically grew back and became whole again. Weeks had passed and Connla craved nothing more than to greet the maiden he had seen that day on *Usna*.

On the last day of the month, all during which Connla ate only from the enchanted apple, he stood by his father on the Plain of Arcomin. As they stood there, his eyes once again caught sight of the magical woman who had been cast away only a month earlier. The King and his guard did not react to the sight of her arrival, as before, until she gently spoke.

"Connla, your place among the mortal men is blessed and one of glory indeed! Mortals are short of life and it is spent awaiting death, but now I beg of you to come. The one who gives life, the ever-living ones – they bid you leave with me. Come to *Moy Mell*, come to the Plain of Pleasure; they have waited long to meet with you and have watched you among those you love here. They have learned to love you through the love you bestowed to others, dear Connla."

Conn, the king, was taken aback when he heard the voice of that same maiden who attempted to steal his son away before. He cried out to his men and said, "Go swiftly and summon Coran, my druid! Today the magical woman has regained her power of speech!"

"Oh, mighty Conn, fighter of the Hundred Fights," said the maiden to the king. "The power of your druid holds no respect any longer in this land. In the land of the mighty, it holds no sway whatsoever, for in *that* land it is filled with people of upright status and minds."

She continued, speaking to the king and his men, "The Law shall come, Conn the king, and when it does, the druid's magic shall be done away with, as will all spells that come from the lips of the false demons!"

It was then that Conn realized he had heard naught from his son since the woman's voice again rang out.

The king turned to his son and asked, "Does your mind lean towards what this woman is saying, my son?"

"This is weighing so very heavy upon me, father," Connla replied, his burden proving his words. "I love my kin, all these folk, and yet… and yet, father, there is a deep longing in me that pulls towards what this maiden has said."

Hearing this, the maiden cried out in reply, "Your longing is stronger than the pull of the oceans, dear Connla. Come with me in my swift *curragh*; my gleaming, sleek, magical vessel. Soon enough we shall reach the realm of King Boadag."

She paused for a brief moment, letting Connla look towards the horizon. "We can see the sun, once bright, is now sinking; yet we can still make our destination before the darkness falls. There, such as you found here, is another land worthy of your journey." Connla turned towards the men and his father before hopping into the craft.

All the king's men watched next to their king as the ship made a straight line across the waters towards a brighter sea. The setting sun seemed to beckon to the small boat as it disappeared, away from where man's eye could see.

And so it was that Connla and the Fairy Maiden went their way – together – on towards the sea. Never to be seen again.

Chapter Seven:

The Changeling

There once was a woman named Mary Scannell. Mary was an ordinary woman who lived with her husband in a large castle – the Castle Martyr – where they had both happily resided for numerous years together. Her husband governed over many fields in which Mary often helped oversee, especially when the harvesting season drew near.

Mary had a young child whom she loved with all of heart, and it was said that never was one without the other. One day she set off to the fields to prepare the harvest. After a time, the workers desired an extra pair of hands to bind the wheat. They hollered and hurried Mary over to help, and so she wrapped her child in her cloak and hid him in the corner of the field. Though she didn't want to leave him, Mary promised to only be gone a moment and, with a kiss on the cheek, she rushed off to lend a hand with the harvest.

It hadn't been long and she had no reason to worry, but when Mary pulled back her cloak to see the face of her child, she felt her breath catch in her chest. This was not the child she had left, but instead was a small, inhuman, cruelly grinning thing!

The moment she revealed its face the creature let out an otherworldly shriek and continued crying despite all her attempts to quieten it. Muffling as best she could with the cloak, she hurried off so that no one else dared know what had just transpired. As she passed, people would fawn over the thing while she muffled the awful cries with the cloak it was wrapped in.

"What a lovely child. *My* lovely child," she would say as crowds passed. In a hurry, Mary sought to find the wise woman of the town to know what to do. Though her voice was of cheer, her heart was dark and fearful of this wicked thing that had taken the place of her beloved child. Clutching the small beast to her chest, she fought back tears thinking of her baby lost somewhere in a world of these creatures.

When she finally came to the house of the wise woman, she was given strict instructions on how to treat this thing that had switched itself in place of her child.

"Follow these words well, and do not stray from them no matter how the thing cries out," the wise woman said, peering warily at the creature in the cloak. "Feed it next to nothing, and when it cries out in hunger, beat and pinch it all the more. Continue this without end, for you must make this thing hate its new home, and desire nothing more than to be switched back with your child!"

Mary nodded, for strange as the instructions were, worse still was imagining a life without her child.

So Mary Scannell took the cloak-wrapped thing home and for a week she fed it the bare minimum, beat it, and pinched it without mercy.

From sunrise to sunset, she made it her mission to pester and frustrate the awful little beast, but each passing morning her child was still nowhere to be seen.

On the eighth day of this wretched schedule, Mary woke to find that the awful shrieking had ceased. Turning to her side, she wept out in joy to find her gorgeous, smiling baby lying there as if nothing had ever happened.

From that day forward Mary never saw that horrible creature, for she had succeeded in making her home a terrible, painful place, and so it wished to never experience such horrors again.

Conclusion

Every branch of mythology and lore speaks with its own language, and the Irish and Celtic ones are no different. From the wildness of the land to the mischievous *good people*, the true nature of the tales remain intact throughout the centuries.

This brief journey of yours through another kind of place is only the beginning as the realm stretches far and wide with immortals, beasts, heroes, and courage! Let the spark that these stories started burn bright as you dive into other areas and cultures to see what those entail.

The world is big, but the world of mythology is bigger.

Happy exploring!

www.ingramcontent.com/pod-product-compliance
Lightning Source LLC
Chambersburg PA
CBHW070104120526
44588CB00034B/2249